MW00966835

MILNE'S MUSINGS

IN PROSE AND POETRY, A PRAIRIE PREACHER PONDERS LIFE AND ITS MEANINGS, DEATH AND RESURECTION

Rev. Don Milne B.A. M.S.T.

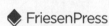 FriesenPress

Suite 300 - 990 Fort St
Victoria, BC, V8V 3K2
Canada

www.friesenpress.com

ISBN
978-1-03-910220-0 (Hardcover)
978-1-03-910219-4 (Paperback)
978-1-03-910221-7 (eBook)

1. Religion, Christianity

Distributed to the trade by The Ingram Book Company

TABLE OF CONTENTS

INTRODUCTION

It is a privilege to have been asked by Don to provide an introduction to this collection of writings. I have such fond remembrances of meeting Don over breakfast at a hotel in Saskatoon. Stuck across the table from two members of the clergy, I was prepared to endure the typical ministerial shoptalk. The minister on the right was going on and on about churches served, religious luminaries known, and academic achievements. In an effort to include Don in this one-way conversation, I asked which churches he had served. Don quietly responded that he had been at the same church, Westview in Yorkton, for the past thirty years, and my heart swelled.

As an interim minister, I know how very difficult it is to pastor for a significant period of time, through all the trials, tribulations, financial uncertainties, and vagaries of church life. You must be able to constantly return to that well of living water to bring hope, healing, and comfort to both yourself and your flock. Stable ministry is an achievement of both a pastor and the flock. Little did I know that after our first chance meeting, I would run into Don on a variety of occasions, including a board meeting, a bus ride, a phone call and eventually as an interim, inherit to his pulpit and office for two years. I certainly didn't envision Don retiring to Regina where my spouse would make his acquaintance.

Saskatchewan born and bred, Don writes about his history with a broad stroke of the pen and then gets down to tell the first-person narrative of the willow tree he planted and nurtured in a beautifully exquisite short story. The religious, mediative poetry is a fine example of the spiritual struggles we all face in life. In all these reflections Don brings the quiet passion, empathy, and certitude of the unseen presence of God

Molly Kitchen

DEDICATION

Unless you have spent time in and around our home, you wouldn't know how much I owe to Sylvia, my wife, since the 11 of July 1956 when we pledged our love and loyalty.

Sylvia, remember we had two ministers conducting our marriage service. At the reception, they both spoke. One told you how to be a minister's wife, and the other spoke to you but about being Don's wife. You took the second one's advice, and in doing that, you have been a tremendous partner and support. Sylvia, you are friendly and approachable and were told things about the church and the community that I needed to know. To thank you in a small way, I dedicate this book to you.

PREFACE

While sitting in our car, I was musing about the first story in this book. How would I begin? A person's first impression often decides if they like a book or not. Then an idea struck me, like a lightning bolt out of the blue. *Milne, you silly old fool, let the tree tell her story.* I did, and the story seemed to tell itself.

Jillian, one of our granddaughters, and Craig Buium were having their marriage service on December 31 2011. Most of the family would be there, and Sylvia, my wife, arranged a family dinner on the 28 of December. She read Silver's Story, and there was not a dry eye in the room. Then there was a special treat for our family.

On September 1, 1980, Saskatchewan turned seventy-five years old. Our government asked the churches to do something special. I decided to write a sort of highlight history. It was used in place of a sermon in Westview United Church in Yorkton on September 7, 1980. *Yorkton This Week* and *Enterprise* asked to print it. I also used it on June 14, 1981 Orkney United Church's annual service. This was a rural church built of local field-stone in 1894. We later moved into College Park Retirement Residence in Regina on October 4, 2011. After a couple of weeks, they asked if I could take a service in the chapel. Looking over my material on the Saskatchewan story, I saw that I had missed some important events. I rewrote it and called it "Saskatchewan: A Half-Hour History." Did I time it? No, but I liked the "h" alliteration.

We often treat animal stories as being fictional. Ask any prairie person if they knew anyone who got caught in a blizzard while driving a team of horses, and they would say they just let the reins go slack, letting the horses choose the track. A lot of people would not have survived if not for those "dumb" animals. Sylvia had something to say about how humans claim total superiority. This next story, "Hitching A Ride," is a true story.

"Will There Ever Be Room" was written for a family Christmas Eve service. The background comes from the story of Mary and Joseph, who could find no room but a crude cattle shelter, and another passage called "The Last Judgement," Matthew 25, 31-46. I wrote it to encourage children of all ages to examine their gift giving and service to help others.

I had never dealt with Simon of Cyrene in Bible study or a sermon, nor had any of my friends. I made Simon a Jew going for his long-planned Passover meal. By carrying the cross, he became unclean, so he could not participate in the Passover. I used Simon to tell the accounts of the crucifixion to his grandson, Simon.

If I were really pressured into choosing a theme for these musings, it would have to be the title of this first piece of poetry. We go, then, to the two birth narratives in the second chapter of Luke and Matthew. I try hard to follow the scriptures—Luke having shepherds visit the baby in the manger, just as the Angel told them. No other people are mentioned. People can imagine lots of things; they come from imagination, as Joseph, midwife, came from my musings.

When we moved to Regina, we had to sell our house and Silver, the old willow tree. Sylvia and I both were assessed by home care, and I needed more care. One morning, my home care aid was late and obviously upset. When I asked her what was wrong, she told me her best friends' husband had committed suicide that morning. We talked about suicide and the feelings that it arouses. When she left, I shared her story with Sylvia and went down for breakfast, but I couldn't get her off my mind. I went back to the suite and started typing. The words seemed to flow, and I didn't have trouble with the rhyme. I sometimes find it is easier to deal with difficult emotions through poetry. I finished the poem "Through the Eyes of Love" and found the home care worker still in the building. I gave her the poem, and she took it to her mother, who bought some better stationary and typed it out. She then shared it with her friend. It was read at the man's funeral.

Rev. Orville Kaminski was a Lutheran pastor who moved into our building. He shared the services in the chapel with me. He had a nephew commit suicide in Calgary around the same time as the home care aid's friend's husband had. I asked for permission to share the poem. I gave it to Orville. When he came back from Calgary, he said it was helpful and came back with a title from a line of one of the verses. He also added the last verse. I have shared this poem with several people since then, and it has been printed in the Folklore in Saskatchewan History magazine.

My mother-in-law, before Sylvia and I even announced our engagement, collected children's stories. One was about two farmers: the rich farmer sending letters in green, blue, and gold envelopes to a poor farmer down in the valley. I used that story in places I served and in Yorkton several times over my thirty years of serving there. I decided to make it into a narrative poem, so "A Tale of Two Farmers" came into being.

"Water From Our Well" is not in any way religious, but it is a true story.

In "Thanksgiving! How?" I've tried to imitate Job's poetry section. I wrote it with two voices. It was well received in both Westview United in Yorkton and at the chapel here in College Park. My son Dale was asked to take a service in their church in Winnipeg. An elderly parishioner told her friend, who was in palliative care, and she asked Dale to mail her a copy. Dale took one over to her right away. Before we had returned home, she had phoned to thank him for his kindness.

"Christ's Last Temptation" I consider to be my best writing to date. When Jesus said, "I am thirsty," I had Jesus move from "My God, my God, why have you forsaken me?" to "It is finished; into your hands I commit my spirit." Jesus said, "When you do kindness to another person, you do it to me." I believe that a preacher should also be a good reader and a listener.

My father served in the trenches of World War I, and two brothers and two brothers- in- law served in World War II. Some ministers and priests do not have this connection and struggle with Remembrance Day. If you want to follow in a prophet's footsteps, the Old Testament prophets would be good ones to follow; they were very political.

A lot of people base their theology on hymns—the words must reveal our contemporary theology. "God reveal your presence," found in a new hymn book, is a prayer to God. When we look at an older hymn book title, the opening line is, "God reveals His presence," which is a statement of belief about God's actions. The gender and language are an issue. "O God of vast creation," was written for a colleague Rev. Irving Fraser for a hundredth anniversary of a church he served. Later that year I revised it for Orkney United Churches hundredth anniversary celebration.

In Luke 19: 40, when Jesus was rebuked by the pharisees for the crowd praising God and Him, Jesus answered, "I tell you that if they keep quiet the stones themselves will start shouting." This was the inspiration for the second hymn that I have included in this work.

I believe that God is not male or female but that we get our femaleness and our maleness from our Creator. Another Hymn, "Faith of our Fathers," now has four verses: faith of our mothers, sisters, and brothers, as well.

My first mission field was at Crane Valley. I was preaching at Davyroyd, Cardross, and Crane Valley. Mrs. Gertrude Ward was the pianist in the Cardross hall, her daughter Donna was just starting high school. Imagine my surprise when Donna and her husband Vernon Brown, were active in the congregation at Westview United in Yorkton. They had a son who they named Ward, and he went on to have a daughter named Shantel. She was a beautiful little girl who contracted a serious illness that left her dependent on life support at fourteen months of age. Ward and his wife, Connie, decided that this was no life for her and for their son, Leighton. I had the funeral service for Donna's granddaughter Shantel, which I have chosen to include. They asked me to stay with Leighton, who was about three or four, while they went to Regina to shut down the machines. Leighton and I played with his tricycle and wagon, hauling gravel. The wagon was a symbol of what was happening to his sister. Without the tricycle, the wagon would not move. They asked if the poem I wrote could be engraved on her head stone. Of course, I said they could, and it is on her marker in the Yorkton memorial gardens. This sermon and poem is included with the families permission.

STORIES

Silver Willow's Story

My name is Silver, and I am a member of the Willow family. No records were kept, so I do not know where I was born or the place from which I originated. My earliest recollection is being in the garden of Ray and June Loe, who lived on the corner of Dogwood Crescent and Mountview Road in Yorkton. I often wonder if the Loe's liked me, because one day Ray dug me up and carried me over to 69 Crestwood Crescent, also in Yorkton. I overheard Ray say to June that he was taking me over to the new manse, because he chaired the Manse Building Committee. He said that the new minister at Westview United Church, Don Milne, had moved into the house with his wife, Sylvia, and their children, Cheryl, Dale, and Doug, on July 21, 1969.

Don dug a small hole in which he planted me. He gave me a big drink of water and packed the earth firmly around my roots. I felt comfortable there, comfortable enough to put down roots. Of course, Don was a mere man, and planted me too close to the house, completely forgetting that I would tower above the house, which was the highest house on the block, standing one and a half stories above the ground.

My first thought was, *I think I'll like it here. The mother's name is similar to mine, the kids leave me alone to grow, and the father keeps me watered.* I quickly started to put down new roots to anchor myself in the ground. But then disaster struck in the form of a fierce prairie hailstorm. My three shoots, which had started to stand proud and tall, were beaten down to the ground. How that hurt! But I couldn't give up. After all, I am a proud member of the resilient Willow family. I sent up some new shoots along with the old ones. I sent up nine in all, but most of them were twisted and bent because of the storm.

As I grew and grew, I wished that the birds would sit on my branches, but Doug's Siamese cat Tammy kept the birds away. When that cat died, the neighborhood felines came to patrol my branches, staking out their favorite places to sun themselves. The birds wouldn't come to nest or even sit on my branches.

One by one the children disappeared, leaving only the mother and father. I was lonely, oh so lonely! And it was so quiet, I wished for children because trees and kids have so much fun together.

Then one winter, I think it was 1980, I heard the sounds of a baby crying in the house. I learned that Cheryl had a baby and called him Aaron, and I could hardly wait for him to grow big enough to climb among my branches. I underwent an extra growth spurt, so that I would be ready for him. What a thrill it was when Don (Aaron called him Pop) sat Aaron on one of my branches and had him pretend to be riding a horse. Soon he was climbing all over my crisscrossed branches. Humans would say that I welcomed him with open arms, but they would be wrong, because I have no arms only limbs. I often wondered who he imagined himself to be as he climbed to the lofty heights. What did he pretend to be doing?

Then a little girl appeared and I heard Aaron say, "Hurry up, Jillian! Hurry up and grow so that we can play together in this willow tree. She grew and grew and on one visit she sat on my branches. I like to think that he wanted a tree-mate with whom to share his fun. Then the two of them asked Don to make a tire swing from one of my stronger, lower branches. Soon a rope was tied around one of my limbs and an old tire tied to the other end. The magnificent sound of laughter would surround me as they played on that swing, swinging back and forth, back and forth.

In 1984, the father got sick and was rushed to Regina, leaving me alone most of the time. During the winter, I heard him talk of building a deck near where I lived. I heard him say that he needed to prove that he was still capable. When summer came, the first thing to go was the tire swing. When Aaron and Jillian came from Regina, I can still remember their angry words: "Why, Pop, why? Why did you take our swing away? How could you do that to us?

You didn't need that stupid, stupid deck!" I'll bet that Don can still hear those words ringing in his ears! I can because those angry words cut into my heart.

Soon another two climbers came to have fun in my branches. I heard Jillian and Aaron call them Meghan and Karyn, as they spurred those youngsters to climb higher and higher. I found out that Meghan was a sister to Aaron and Jillian, and that Karyn was Dale's first daughter. By this time, the older kids were proficient climbers. I called them my aerial acrobats. Then came a pair of sisters for Karyn: Katrina in 1985 and Jennifer a year later, but before they could hug me, their family moved to Regina. I could have been called the Weeping Willow, because I was so sad. The only time my friends came to visit me was when they came to visit the old people who were now called Grandma and Pop. But those older two must still have liked me because twice Sylvia and Cheryl sent the old man to the paint store to try to match the color of my leaves on the branches that towered over the house. They wanted to paint the panels at the front entrance. I overheard a neighbor, Merv Laube, comment on how closely the panels matched my leaves.

Sometimes in the summer, I would have Doug's children, Scott, Brett, and Kelly, come to visit me. I didn't get to know them as I did the other six that I have told you about. Most times I heard my people say that they were coming to the lake. How I disliked that place, wherever it was! I heard that Cheryl married Ken, giving my people three more grand-children, Dore, Kara, and Levi, but they were too big to play with me.

I also heard Don say that someone had called me a self-pruning tree. I lost a lot of little branches in even a gentle breeze, and I lost a lot of big branches when the wind blew hard. I am grateful to Sylvia, because she stuck up for me after a severe summer storm had torn me limb from limb. I heard Don say that he wanted to cut me down, because he was concerned I might fall on the house. If that wasn't suffering enough, another storm ripped me apart again, leaving my branches scattered all over the lawn. I had lost so many branches that Ken almost filled three dumpsters with my debris. He would have, too, if he hadn't cut my branches into little pieces. Looking back, I often wonder at how I survived the loss of so many limbs. Thank you, God, for the resilience of the Willow clan.

I had a very thrilling moment when Meghan came one summer, all dressed in white. It was June 27, 2009, her wedding day, and she wanted pictures taken with me. Just imagine that—a pretty young girl, glowing as only a bride can glow, wanting pictures with me, a gnarled, misshapen old tree. I was so thrilled that I shook with excitement and happiness.

Don found some rot at the bottom of two of my trunks and finally convinced Sylvia that they had to amputate two of my limbs that were over twenty inches in diameter. Cheryl came to my rescue and said that if we cut off my limbs, they needed to have a wood carver release the spirits that were an inner part of me. My people contacted Rory Stachiw of Emerald Arts. Rory lived in Wishart, Saskatchewan, and was a professional wood carver—a real artist. So, I lost those two limbs, with Rory taking all the wood. At the base of one of my stumps, my people found a heart—a heart that showed my love for them. Don claimed it, saying that it was his valentine for Sylvia. How wrong he was, but then, humans like to take credit for everything!

Then I found out that my humans were selling their house and me, and were moving to Regina. I was so sad because they were the only family I ever had. and I cried when Jillian said "goodbye house, goodbye willow" and I waved goodbye to her knowing I would never see her again. I was glad that my humans would have not just memories of me, but also my spirits, released by Rory as he carved them from the two limbs that he had taken.

I also heard that Jillian was getting married and that they were having a family dinner two days before her wedding. I was told that Rory had taken fifteen of my spirits to Sylvia and Don in Regina, and that each of their children and grandchildren had to pick a spirit, beginning with the oldest and going by age to the youngest. I hope they will treasure their part of me and that it will release the memories of the fun they had with me when they were children. Goodbye my family, goodbye. Please treasure and enjoy my spirit.

Sincerely,

Silver Willow

Saskatchewan: A Half-Hour History

First there was the land—land created by the word of God and then ceaselessly re-formed and re-shaped by those constant natural forces: wind and water. Sometimes the wind blew softly across the land, caressing its surface with a gentle breeze, like the soft whisper of a kiss on a baby's cheek. At other times it roared over the land, carrying in its mighty grip particles of soil or snow, eventually to pile them up in vast drifts.

The water was always there to moisten and enrich the soil, or to beautify the landscape with rivers and streams, lakes and sloughs. But it also changed the face of the land. In the surging monotony of the lap, lap, lap of the waves, pebbles were ground to sand and sand to silt. Rivers cut new channels in their old beds. Melting snow carried some soil away, leaving furrows like the wrinkles etched on an old person's brow by time and tragedy. When the ice came, it crushed and ground and leveled the surface of the land. In its melting retreat, gravel hills and rocky ridges were left behind, and great valleys were carved out by the melted water rushing back to its source: the sea.

When great seas covered the face of the land, deposits of salts and minerals were left on the sea floor and then covered over until centuries later when they would form part of the great wealth of the land. Later, in the warm swampy waters, enormous amounts of vegetation would grow. When that era ended and the dead foliage was covered by sand and soil, it was crushed into coal that people would use to heat their homes and generate electricity. Some of that vegetation was pressed and pressured until oil was formed. In the north, vast deposits of uranium were discovered—a part of the wealth of the land that would generate discussion and controversy over its use.

The first settlers probably came from Asia. They were content to catch fish from the rivers and lakes and kill the bountiful game that roamed wild and free. Moose, elk, antelope, and deer were plentiful, but their main source of food was the shaggy buffalo: the humped-back, ox-like creature that scientists would later call bison. The flesh was eaten fresh or dried, with some pounded with berries to make pemmican. Hides were tanned and sewn into garments and tents. In the treeless prairie, the dung was used to fuel their fires. Little did they change the face of the land, these first human inhabitants, but they learned how to live in this ever-changing land that, at times, was warmly hospitable, graciously bestowing its bounty on human and beast, but at other times could be brutally savage, threatening and taking life in raging winter blizzards.

As their tribes grew, they laid claim to their territories and developed their traditions. Dance became an important part of the preparation for battle with neighboring tribes or for the hunt. It was also part of their celebration and thanksgiving after a successful battle or hunt. And in all their ceremonies, the Creator, whom some tribes called Gitchi Manitou, was the god to approach in supplication and in gratitude.

When Europeans first saw this land, they were not interested in it but rather a way through it. The western sea beckoned them, and the fabled lands of the Orient were so often on their minds that they did not see the wealth they walked over. The First Nations people helped them to survive in this land of extremes. They fed them when they were starving, nursed them in their sickness, and welcomed them into their homes and families. When Europe hungered for furs and pelt, these men saw the vast potential of this western land, fighting each other for the right to trade trinkets, guns, knives, and whiskey for the furs of the First Nations. The white men went on wanton killing sprees, exterminating the vast herds of buffalo for their hides, leaving their flesh to rot and their bones to bleach in the scorching summer sun. These bones would be gathered and piled for sale later, when they were shipped to the east to be ground to make gunpowder and fertilizer. Even in those early years, the raw materials of the west would be sent east to the processing houses and manufacturing plants. Regina would first be called "Pile of Bones," because of the enormous piles of buffalo bones awaiting shipment to the east.

The virtual extermination of the buffalo drastically changed the way of life of the First Nations people and the Metis. They had been semi-nomadic, following the herds till they had a successful hunt. Many of the Metis had become freighters, transporting goods by ox-cart from one trading post to another. The building of the railroad gradually took away this source of money. Those who were farmers held their land in narrow strips that fronted on the rivers, mainly on the North and South Saskatchewan.

As is mentioned later, there was real conflict over land ownership when the surveyors came with their square mile plan. The major area of conflict was around Batoche and Duck Lake, and eventually they called on Louis Riel to come out of exile in Montana to assist them. He had led an uprising in the Red River Colony north of Winnipeg in the postage stamp province of Manitoba, had established a provisional government, and had declined an offer of help from the Governor of Minnesota. He had also been elected as a Member of Parliament but was rebuffed, and the Canadian government would not let him take his seat in Parliament. These facts may not be in chronological order, but they resulted in him fleeing to Montana.

He came to the Batoche area on June 27, 1884 and led what historians call the Riel Rebellion. Gabriel Dumont was to be the military commander. If Riel, who was always deeply religious, had developed some almost insane ideas and left Dumont alone, the results may have been different. Many meetings were held but to no avail. A provisional government was set up with Riel as President, and he told five priests, "The Provisional Government is declared, and we have five prisoners already. The old Roman Woman [the Pope in Rome] is broken. I have a new Pope in the person of Bishop Bourget of Montreal. From now on, you will be priests of the new religion, and you will obey me." The war started on March 26 with the shooting of Isadore Dumont, Gabriel's brother, and an unarmed First Nations person, Assiywin, who had come to negotiate with the police. The last battle was fought on or around May 12, 1885.

Some treaties had been signed between the First Nations peoples and the representatives of the Queen. Big Bear, Chief of the Plains Cree, had settled with his band near the Alberta settlement at Frog Lake. He tried to negotiate with neighboring tribes and with the Indian Agent, Thomas Quinn, because he was a peaceful man. No buffalo, no game, and an agent who was reluctant to issue adequate food supplies—these were all sources of irritation, unrest, and desperate moves. When Big Bear was out on a hunting trip on the morning of April 2, 1885, the War Chief, Wandering Spirit, led a group of armed men to the agent's house and office. When Quinn refused to go to the Cree camp, Wandering Spirit shot him. In the resulting melee, eight other men were killed. The men took the stores and the Hudson's Bay store apart in a desperate search for food. Some of the Cree women hid the young clerk at the Bay store, William B. Cameron. When Big Bear returned, he was upset, but as Chief he supported his people. He led them, some Metis people, and some captives—the white women of Frog Lake and the clerk, Cameron, the sole male survivor of what some call the Frog Lake Massacre. Others call it the desperate acts of starving people who knew that food was held in the stores of the agent. Cameron gave credit to the Metis men for protecting the women and himself.

Big Bear and Wandering Spirit led the people, and they moved between the present Yellowhead Highway and the North Saskatchewan River, then north around Paradise Hill and Fort Pitt, with the last battle at Steele Narrows near Loon Lake. Neither the Metis nor the First Nations peoples got anything they wanted. Riel and Wandering Spirit were hanged, along with others. Big Bear was imprisoned, and Gabriel Dumont fled to the United States, where it is rumored that he joined a Wild West show. He was later pardoned and returned to Batoche, where he was treated with great respect. He died in the spring of 1906 and was the last link to the 1885 conflict.

The fur traders caused the face of parts of the land to change, a fact that is mostly forgotten. Beavers were trapped to virtual extinction in the wooded north of what we now call Saskatchewan. When the beavers were destroyed, their dams decayed and their ponds dried up, lowering the water table in the ever-thirsty soil. Waterfowl lost their nesting-places, and members of the deer family had to move to find water and food. Even the early fur traders began to change the ecological balance of nature and erode the face of Saskatchewan. In the late 1940s, beaver was live trapped and taken north to the wooded area of the province to form the nucleus of the now thriving beaver colonies and the rejuvenation of the fur trade, restoring an ancient economic resource to some of the First Nations people.

The next settlers were the ranchers, driving their herds of cattle up from the United States and out from the east to pasture them on the prairie wool. Blizzards in the winter and grass fires in the summer were constant threats to their livelihood, forcing them to develop communities of co-operation to strengthen the thin thread that held them from extinction. Old-timers, not so many years ago, told of the cattle drives up from south of the border, the lonely times spent in the saddle, and the frightening times when the herd stampeded, often in all four directions of the compass.

After the ranchers, the farmers came, breaking the land and fencing the prairie. In the northern part, the bush had to be cleared before the land could be broken. Why did they come to this unsettled land of Saskatchewan? The answers were almost as many and as varied as the people who came. Some were lured by the promise of "free" land—only ten dollars and three years of back-breaking labor, and you could own one hundred and sixty acres, a quarter section, of land. That was very appealing to people who would never have been able to own land in their old countries. Some came for the adventure—the old countries were too locked in by tradition for these free spirits. Some came through compulsion—their free spirits had made them unacceptable members of their noble families, and they were paid a regular remittance to stay away from home. Others came for religious reasons—they wanted and were granted freedom to worship God in their own way, a way that was not the common way in the old land.

The English, Irish, and Scottish came out from Upper Canada (Ontario) and the French from Lower Canada (Quebec). Metis settlers came from the postage stamp province of Manitoba to settle on unsurveyed land along the rivers, farming narrow strips back from the river. This became a real irritation when the land was surveyed into sections that were a square mile. Some settlers came from the United States and from all the lands of Europe, from the near East and from the western areas of

Asia. They came with their traditions and customs, eventually to give a hybrid picturesqueness and vigor to Saskatchewan society. They also brought hatred and prejudice fostered by countless generations. But most of all, they brought the hope and dream that life would be better for themselves and even more for their children.

They all faced untold hardships as they carved caves in the hillside to live in; or plowed the prairie sod, cut it into strips, and built sod houses; or cut the virgin timber to build log homes. Some had never really used any tools, let alone a farm equipment to till the soil. They had to rely on the kindness of their neighbors to teach them what to do. Others came with experience, as they had tilled the soil of their homeland. Most of them were willing to share their knowledge with the greenhorns, but as always, there were the unscrupulous who took advantage of the new settlers. Now they all tell of the good old days. Good because they remember the fun, the sharing, the co-operation that lifted their spirits; good because the hardships and the heartaches were forgotten as hope for a better next year sprang eternal in their hearts and minds.

Scarcely had they built their houses when they took time to build their churches and schools. These were more than sanctuaries and classrooms; they were community centers in the truest sense of the word. People who in the old land would have worshiped separately in Anglican, Presbyterian, Roman

Catholic, Greek Catholic, Lutheran, Orthodox, or Methodist churches, in some districts, now joined hands to build the little cathedrals of the plains, the frame or stone churches that dotted the prairie landscape. People who couldn't sign their own name made sure that their children had the opportunity to read and write. Some of these students went on to become the teachers, doctors, nurses, ministers, and priests for the next generation. Those pioneers knew how important it was, and is, to build for the future, even when still struggling in the present.

But the old lands would not leave the new alone. Old desires for power and conquest embroiled Europe in war once more. The young men of Saskatchewan left to fight in the "war to end all wars." People, whatever their background, fought shoulder to shoulder for their new country. Often their bullets and bombs were directed across the battle lines at cousins from the old land. Their new country had called, and with a newfound patriotism, they left their half-broken farms and small-town businesses to rid the world of tyranny and oppression. Back these young men came, made old by the cruelty and barbarism of battle, to face inflation, then a short depression, then another period of inflation. Then the stock market crashed, and the world faced a bitter depression. But in Saskatchewan, the crash of 1929 was accompanied with an event that left an indelible mark on the face of the province and its people, when the rains left and the land that had blossomed like a rose now became a desert. The "Dirty Thirties" struck with a vengeance. It was the "better" farmers who lost the most of their fertile top soil. The prevailing practice was to keep a dust mulch on the top of the summer fallow. Anybody who had trash or weeds were called Indian farmers. The dust mulch was fodder for the relentless wind that piled the fertile soil along fence lines and in the clumps of bush in the parkland area.

After being hailed out, grasshoppered out, and frozen out, the farmers were being dried out. Many left for the north, where the rains still fell, or for the western coast. Some stayed, either out of sheer determination, or because they had nowhere else to go and nothing left to finance their trip out of the Saskatchewan dust bowl.

The constant dust was an annoyance to all. Women, especially those with tiny babies or children with breathing problems, tried keeping the dust out by laying damp cloths on the window sills and wet towels at the edge of the door. It was to no avail. That fine dust filtered in and covered everything. All you had to do was crawl into the attic of one of those houses during that time to see the layers of dust settled there by that relentless wind. Dust storms were like blizzards—you couldn't see. The one difference was the dust, which choked the unfortunate people caught in its path. If the farm managed to produce a crop, it was almost worthless; a bushel of good wheat sold for about eight cents. People who shipped cattle to the slaughter houses were sent a bill.

The animal did not fetch enough to pay the freight. Young people left home, desperately trying to find work. Governments would pay people to create a job for the unemployed. Men "rode the rails," riding in empty box cars or on the roof of those same box cars, trying to avoid the dreaded railway police. Or they walked the dusty roads, stopping at farms and houses in towns, begging for meals. If successful, they would put some mark on the house or the gate so the other hungry fellows who followed them in endless succession would know that in that house lived someone who would share the little that they had with those who had nothing.

The return of the rains brought news of more trouble in Europe—another war. The finest resource that Saskatchewan could ever boast about, her young men and women, volunteered in the thousands. Some served in the armed forces, others in the factories, and others on the farms to produce food. While only a short time before, they couldn't find work for willing hands, now work was available and there were jobs for all and then some.

When the soldiers, sailors, and airmen returned home, society, once again, expected them to fit in as if nothing had happened. Most of them could have been diagnosed as having Post Traumatic Stress Syndrome. But they did fit in, and the face of Saskatchewan was changed dramatically. Many of the pioneers were ready to retire and were waiting for sons and daughters to return to the family farm.

Farms got larger and more mechanized. Power lines were strung across the prairie landscape, bringing the convenience of electricity, long enjoyed by the citizens of the city, to the tiller of the soil and his unsung helpmate and companion, his wife. Now she could freeze fruit and vegetables, meat, bread, and baking and could prepare meals ahead for the busy harvest time. How those pioneer women, who had to cook for the ever-hungry threshing crews as well as do many of the daily chores, would have appreciated those modern conveniences. Combines had done away with the large threshing crews, and often the farm women did as much outside work as the men. And when the economy took a bad turn, one or the other had to take an off-farm job.

Country schools were closed because of the sparsity of pupils, due to larger farms. Economically, five schools could be bussed into a central school for the cost of four. Instead of walking up to three miles to school, the big yellow bus picked the pupils up at their home. Highways were being paved or oiled and a grid road system was started. Having lost their reason for being, small towns disappeared or became ghost towns. More people were living in the cities, even though agriculture was still number one in the provincial economy. Then oil was discovered, and even though our reserves were not like Alberta's, it was the beginning of the change in the province's economy. While drilling exploratory holes, potash was discovered—a legacy from the time that much of the province was a vast inland sea. Soon potash mines covered the central part of the populated area. A mighty dam was built at Outlook, and the age-old dream of harnessing the South Saskatchewan River to produce electricity and provide water for irrigation became a reality.

Saskatchewan has more kilometers of roads than any other province, partly because the surveyors made provision for a north-south road every mile and an east-west road every two miles. That makes a block containing two sections of land, each of which has six hundred and forty acres. Each section was divided into four quarters, each containing one hundred and sixty acres. Regina and Saskatoon were the two major cities competed for the Legislature and the University. Regina was given the Legislature, and a beautiful building was erected. During the 1930s, Wascana Lake was dug, enlarging the creek by the same name and providing a beautiful setting for the Legislature. The University of Saskatchewan was built in Saskatoon, with all the original buildings built of native prairie stone. In the pioneer days, the Methodist Church established Regina College, and it eventually grew into the University of Regina. Because of the nature of our soil and the extreme changes in temperature, roads and buildings required more maintenance and upkeep. That is the reason why Saskatchewan doesn't have a lot of old buildings.

Saskatchewan people are very co-operative and have established many co-op enterprises. In the early

1920s, many municipalities hired their own doctor, and anyone living in the municipality had access to the doctor's services without extra payment. That was an early introduction to Medicare, so it is not surprising that we had the first hospitalization plan and Medicare plan, which now covers all of Canada. Crown corporations own and distribute natural gas and power, and provide telephone service.

That is some of Saskatchewan's past and present: a part of the heritage that we have as citizens of this province, which was established by an Act of the Parliament of Canada, taking effect on September 1, 1905, carved out of the Northwest Territories, as was Alberta and a larger Manitoba. Whether you are a pioneer, an old-timer, a native daughter or son born in this province, or a recent immigrant to our province—whether from another province or territory, or another land—join us in celebrating our past and in planning for our future, because as the song says, "This land is your land; this land is my land." Think of the history of the First Nations people, the fur traders, the explorers and map makers, the ranchers and farmers, and all the pioneers who came before; think of what they accomplished and the legacy they left. Remember the teachers in little one-room schools and in the universities and colleges. Don't forget the lessons you learned from your family, the neighbor down the street, and all the people you have met, for we can learn from everybody and anybody. Think of the beauty of our Saskatchewan landscape from Roche Percee to the Cypress Hills, from the prairie over that stretches the endless sky to the forests of poplar and spruce, birch and pine and celebrate Saskatchewan!

Hitching A Ride

We tend to discount animal stories as being fictional, but "Hitching A Ride" is a true story that I witnessed personally. I had driven to Winnipeg to attend a Parkinson's disease meeting. Our son Dale picked me up after the meeting, and we went back to his home. He and his wife lived on the Eastern banks of the Red River, which flows through Winnipeg, Manitoba. Dale had embarked on the task of replacing his back deck, and the I thought I would lend a hand.

That spring had an unusually quick thaw, and with the extreme amount of snow that had fallen in the Red River valley that past winter, the Red was running extremely high, even with the flood gates activated. It was a sight to see, with the fast-flowing current running North through Lockport and on to Lake Winnipeg. The flotsam and jetsam were constant. We would see numerous trees and branches that had been sheared off by the ice, as well as pieces of docks and any number of objects that had washed from people's property downstream.

My son's property sat on a straight spot on the river, directly across from the University of Manitoba. At one point in the morning, I saw a particularly curious sight. Coming around the south bend was a very large log, and on each end of the log stood a sandhill crane: one standing watch at the front and the captain at the back. I immediately thought of the old National Film Board vignette of the log rollers and could hear the song in my head. I watched, fascinated, as the pair rode their log until it was about to disappear around the next bend to the north. Suddenly, both cranes took flight and found another large tree that was coming around the south bend. The larger crane, who had been in the bow of the last log, took the stern on the new log. The smaller crane took the bow, and the two of them rode the new log north. Once again, as it rounded the north bend up, they flew in search of the next log. This continued for several minutes, each time the birds switching positions on the logs and seeming to enjoy the ride down the mighty Red River.

I remember this sight to this day, and for anyone who says that animals don't have a sense of play or joy, I challenge your thinking. Clearly those two sandhill cranes were playing in the river and thoroughly enjoying themselves, not to mention the joy they gave this old man watching from the shore.

Will There Ever Be Room?

The western sky was bathed in a soft, warm red glow, left behind by the setting sun. There was a nip of frost in the air, giving a foretaste of winter. An old man shuffled slowly down the street, pausing at every street corner to look left and right. As we watched him, he showed all the signs of being lost. At one corner, he heard the sound of children playing happily outside in the twilight. His steps quickened as he turned to walk toward the sound. One boy, who looked about eight years old, was hiding behind some shrubbery. When the old man saw him, a relieved smile bathed his tired face. "Sonny," he said, "can you help me? My car broke down, and I left it at a garage. I decided to walk to the motel, but I must have taken a wrong turn, and now I'm lost. Could you show me the way to the motel where I can spend the night and wait till my car is fixed?"

"No, I won't," the boy whispered. "Can't you see that I'm busy playing hide and seek with my friends. If I talk too long with you, they might hear me and find me. If I told you, you'd forget and probably get lost again. Gee, I think I can get home-free now." The boy ran off, leaving the old man alone, still bewildered and wondering which way to go.

Click-swish, click-swish, click-swish. The sound marked the slow progress of a teenager walking down the sidewalk. The clicks were made by his arm crutches, as he swung them ahead to take the next step. The swish was the sound of his left foot being dragged along the sidewalk. Click-swish, click-swish, click-swish. A car coming down the street behind him was filled with teenage boys. They were headed for a drive-in to have something to eat after football practice. "Hey, there's Mark," one of the boys said. "Maybe we should give him a ride. It must be pretty hard carrying himself down the street with nothing much but his shoulder muscles." They all knew Mark. He was in their class at school, but his crippled left leg and crutches kept him from joining in their sports and games. Besides, he was always first in the class; his marks were better than theirs. "Let's stop and give him a ride. Besides, he is never with anyone else and must be so lonely."

But the driver answered, "No, there's just not enough room. We'd have to double up if he came into the car, and he and those crutches would take up too much room."

The boy in the front passenger seat added, "We don't know where he is going, and he's used to walking like that; he does it all the time." The boy who had suggested stopping never said another word in support of Mark. The boys passed Mark, without so much as a wave, driving off and leaving Mark on the sidewalk, click-swishing his slow walk down the street.

A group of happy girls came giggling out of the school. School was out for the day, and they were enjoying their freedom and friendship. One of the girls said, "Look, there's Tan. Should we ask her to come play with us?"

"Why should we? She's never tried to be friendly to us," was one reply.

Another girl said, "'Tan', now that is a funny name. Makes me think of what happens to my skin when I go to the beach in the summer. But maybe that is a good name for a yellow-skinned girl." The rest of the girls all tittered and giggled. "My dad says they shouldn't even be in this country. Why didn't they stay in Vietnam where they belong?"

The girls hopped and skipped their way down the street, ignoring the little girl who stood shy and alone on the edge of the school playground, her yellow skin and jet-black hair making her different. Then, sadly, she turned and walked away to her home above the café that her parents operated.

The house stood apart from all of the others, separated from them by size and grandeur as much as by distance. It was so much bigger than the others. It was well-kept with neat lawns and shrubbery. A neatly trimmed hedge rimmed the property, letting people know that this house and yard were special and reflecting that the occupants had class. Tonight, the house was well lit, both inside and out, and it was surrounded by cars. It didn't take much to know that there was a party going on inside. Let's invite ourselves as unseen guests, so that we may know what is happening. The house is owned by a successful young businessman and his very beautiful wife. Look at the furniture—beautiful, isn't it? Their clothes and those of their guests all showed that they were well on their way up the ladder of success. They were all enjoying themselves, eating, drinking, talking, and laughing. Then the hostess called everyone to the dining room, where the dinner was being served.

The soup had just been served when the doorbell rang. The maid answered it. The hostess wondered who it could be. Is it some guest arriving late, coming after the cocktails and *hors d'oeuvres* have been served and the meal started? No. All the place-names had been carefully and strategically placed around the massive table, and every chair was taken. The maid came in and whispered something in the hostess' ear. A frown flicked over the hostess' brow, and she whispered some instructions to the maid. Let's eavesdrop to hear what she is saying.

"Tell them that they will have to ask someone else. They have their nerve interrupting me. They could see that we have guests and are too busy."

The maid left, returning to remove the soup dishes and serve the rest of the meal. After some cards and drinks, the guests all left, thanking their hosts for a delicious meal and a most enjoyable evening.

When the couple were settled in their bed, the husband asked, "Who was at the door, and what did the maid say to you? I saw a frown flicker across your face. I would like to know what troubled you."

She answered, "Oh, it was the Smiths, who live a few doors down the street. Their little girl was sick. Their car wouldn't start, the bus wasn't running, and they didn't want to call a taxi—they probably thought that it was too much money. Imagine the nerve of some people, asking if someone here would drive them to the hospital. They could see that we were entertaining and should have known that we couldn't leave."

Time passed. Christmas Eve came, and the television sets were tuned in to a service. The familiar story of Jesus' birth was read, ending with, "There was no room for them to stay in the inn." A little boy heard those words and thought about the lost old man. He should have helped him find his way to the motel. Was getting home-free more important than helping someone find a place to stay? He had been so rude to a lost and confused old man who had asked so nicely for his help.

Several teenage boys heard those words and remembered when there was no room in their car for Mark and his crutches, leaving him to click-swish his lonely way down the street. He must hurt all the time. They could have helped . . . at least they could be his friend.

Some little girls heard those words, as they sat with their families. Each one thought of the little Vietnamese girl, Tan, and how sad and lonely she looked when they went giggling by. They should make room for her.

In a beautiful house on the edge of town, a couple heard those words—no room! Had their guests been so important that one of them couldn't spare a little time to drive their sick young neighbors and her distraught parents to the hospital?

"They laid him in a manger. There was no room for them to stay in the inn." That baby grew, and as a man he said that when you have shown kindness, friendship, and love to any of His sisters and brothers, you have shown it to Him.

Simon and Simon:
A Grandson-Grandfather
Dialogue

Simon Junior (SJ): Grandpa, you know that I have been studying as a catechumen for this past year. I have questions that I hesitate to ask our leader. You have always answered my questions and treated me as an equal. Can I ask you my questions?

Simon Senior (SS): I am pleased that you are studying, and yes, I will answer any questions that I can.

SJ: Why are we Christians? There are more Jews in Cyrene. I heard Mom and Dad say that you began your life as a Jew. Why did you become a Christian?

SS: I had a chance encounter with Jesus that changed my whole life. Before that, I was a devout Jew.

SJ: Tell me all about it. I want to hear the whole story.

SS: Maybe you know that every devout Jew wants to spend at least one Passover in Jerusalem. I had planned my trip for years. When I was thirty, I left a month before Passover, because it is a long and dangerous journey through deserts and wild wilderness where savage animals prowl and robbers prey on unsuspecting pilgrims. When we have to take a boat, there are a lot of rough, stormy seas. We reached the outskirts of Jerusalem late on a Thursday night, but the city gates had already been closed, so we camped there and entered the city on Friday morning. We started our journey through the city to the Temple, but it was slow going. The streets were full of people, most of whom were shouting, "Crucify him! Crucify him!" I looked down the street and saw a large crowd coming toward us, led by a group of heavily armed Roman soldiers. I thought of going down a side street, but curiosity got the better of me, so I stayed where I was but moved back off the road. Then I saw a condemned man who had obviously been beaten. There were deep scratches on his forehead and rivulets of dried blood all over his head. Hanging around his neck was a notice of the charge for which he was condemned, "This is Jesus, King of the Jews." He was carrying a heavy cross piece. Then he stumbled and fell to his knees. Two of the soldiers grabbed him, yanking him to his feet. I didn't notice it, but two other soldiers had come through the crowd and grabbed me by the arms, pulling me to Jesus. They took the cross bar from Jesus and made me carry it.

SJ: Grandpa, what did you think of that? What did you feel?

SS: I was angry. Now I was unclean and couldn't go into the temple. My dream of eating the Passover meal was shattered and all because of that man. I looked at him, giving him the angriest glare possible. Then he looked at me. Oh, Simon, if you could only have seen his eyes. I saw gratitude and his thankfulness for what I was doing. But even more, his eyes told me that he knew me through and through. He knew all of my sins and failures, as well as my hopes and dreams. I felt accepted and forgiven by God. Then I accepted the cross, because I was helping him.

SJ: That is weird, to have such a change in feeling and attitude so quickly. What did you experience next?

SS: I started watching Jesus more closely. The sign said that he was King of the Jews. In spite of the beatings that he'd obviously had, he had an inner regal bearing—a kind of serenity despite his suffering.

SJ: Where were they taking him?

SS: They took him to Golgotha, a place where there had been many crucifixions. The Romans had placed several uprights in the ground. The condemned man was nailed to the cross bar, and they hoisted the bar up, fastening it to the upright.

SJ: The thought of that cruel death makes me sick. I bet you got out of there as soon as the soldiers took the cross bar from you.

SS: No, Simon, I had to stay. Those eyes kept me there. In Cyrene, we had heard rumors about this man, and I had to know more about him.

SJ: You must have been quiet when he was hung on the cross.

SS: No. All the time that I was carrying the cross, the crowd was jeering and taunting him. People were shouting, "He saved others, let him save himself. Save yourself if you are God's son." As he was hanging on the cross, even the priests and teachers of the law made fun of him. They said, "He saved others, but he cannot save himself! Isn't he the king of Israel? If he will come down from the cross now, we will believe in him! He trusts in God and claims to be God's son. Well, then, let us see if God wants to save him now!"

SJ: How did Jesus answer them?

SS: He didn't. On the way to Golgotha, he never said a word. In the over three hours that it took him to die, he only spoke seven times. Some of his sentences reflected his human needs, like "I am thirsty," or "Father, into your hands I commit my spirit." To me, that sounded like a bed-time prayer. Then there was one that came from the depths of his being, revealing the feeling of total abandonment, even and especially by God. He said, "Eloi, Eloi, lema sabach-thani? My God, my God, why did You abandon me?" That was sort of how I felt when they put the cross on my shoulders, and I realized that I was ritually unclean and would miss my Passover.

There were sentences that seemed to spring right out of the heart of God. One was, "Forgive them, Father! They don't know what they are doing." Just think about that, Simon, forgiveness for all those involved in his suffering and death.

There were two others crucified with Jesus. They were common criminals and one said, "Save yourself and us!" But the other criminal said to him, "Don't you fear God? You received the same sentence he did. Ours, however, is only right, because we are getting what we deserve for what we did, but he has done no wrong." He said to Jesus, "Remember me, Jesus, when you come as King!" Jesus said to him, "I promise you that today you will be in paradise with me." Much later he said, "It is finished!"

SJ: What did he mean? Was it that his life was over or that his work was done?

SS: I thought he spoke with a sense of accomplishment, that he had successfully completed what God wanted him to do.

SJ: You have only given me six times he spoke. What is the seventh one?

SS: Some women were standing under the shadow of the cross. One was Jesus' mother. Jesus knew the law allowed his brothers and sisters to refuse to have anything to do with her because she was with their brother who was dying a criminal's death. So, Jesus made an arrangement for his mother to go to his disciple John's house and for John to treat her as his mother. He said to his mother, "He is your son." To John, he said, "She is your mother."

SJ: I can see now why he made such an impression on you, Grandpa. Jesus, while dying such an agonizing death, as concerned about other people. I see why our church places so much emphasis on Good Friday.

SS: But the events of Friday were not the end. I stayed in the city, trying to learn more about Him. Some of his female followers went to the tomb on Sunday morning to find the stone rolled away and the tomb empty. He rose from the dead on Easter morning, on Sunday. We can't have one without the other. We have special days and seasons when we remember aspects of Jesus' life among us humans. But most of all, we remember that behind Jesus' ministry was God—God who so loved the world that he gave his only son, that when we believe in Him we have eternal life.

SJ: Thanks, Grandpa. Why don't you tell your story more often?

SS: The story is about Jesus. I was only the man they forced to carry his cross. I was only the man who had the privilege of carrying his cross.

SJ: You really believe, don't you, Grandpa? Meeting Jesus made you become a Christian.

SS: Yes, Simon, but we have only been called Christians for the last few years. I hope that you will believe, as well. The story of Jesus of Nazareth is the greatest love story in the world. God loved the world so much that he gave his son, so that everyone who believes in Him may not die but have eternal life.

POETRY

Emmanuel, God Is With Us

Christmas is the time to again hear that story,
how through a young maiden, God showed God's glory.
Do not be worried, Mary, have no fear;
in the Holy Spirit God has come near.

You will become pregnant, giving birth to a son.
Through the one that you bear, God's work will be done.
He will be great, his kingdom unending.
Love to the world through you God is sending.

I'm your servant, so now let it be
as you have said, may it be done to me.
So spoke the young Mary in obedient trust,
singing praises to God, merciful and just.

Her words seemed so easy, so full of grace,
but now she had her own people to face—
a people where, with the hard hurled stone,
woman's life can be battered from flesh and bone.

They had their law from Sinai told,
a law that made men in cruelty bold.

At her father›s house, right in front of the door,
they could stone her till she breathed no more.

Mary told Joseph he's not the father.
Of course, Joseph planned now to give Mary a quiet divorce.
But in a dream, he learned what had been done
and that Jesus was the name of the coming one.

A whim of Caesar Augustus in faraway Rome
made Mary and Joseph leave their Nazareth home.
Each family must go to be on the list;
in the name of efficiency no one can be missed.

Each step of the journey made Joseph more harried,
as he saw Mary›s pain from the baby she carried.
In crowded Bethlehem, they find no room at all;
for refuge they go to a crude cattle stall.

There all alone in the dirt in the grime,
away from her helpers, now was Mary›s time.
Alone in this pain that's the hardest to stand.
Alone without the comfort of another woman›s hand.

Pain, when it strikes, takes control of our lives,
blotting out all but its misery and strife.
Alone in that stable Mary had to give birth
to the baby announced as "Lord of the earth."

Calloused hands, familiar with hammer and saw,
must comfort the mother on her bed of straw.
Calloused hands, used to working with wood,
must do all that a midwife should.

Joseph the Carpenter was now the midwife'
trying to aid Mary in the midst of her strife.
Holding her hand when in pain she shrieked,
catching the baby, all wet and blood streaked.

Joseph wrapped the baby in swaddling bands,
made ready before by Mary's loving hands.
Jesus, leaving the safety of his mother's womb,
was born into this world with its waiting tomb.

There was great anguish. Only after it was done
could Mary ponder the gift of her newborn son.
Alone in that stable there's no one to hear
the news of this baby, so precious, so dear.

Out in the country, in the dark of the night,
shepherds were startled as the sky turned bright.
Like Mary and Joseph, they were filled with fear,
but an angel gave them great news to hear.

"Don't be afraid. You must go down
to the old stable in David's town.
In the manger, where you feed your sheep,
you'll find a new baby, fast asleep.

"The child you will see as a tiny baby boy
will be to all people a child of great joy.
Great happiness, now, to all people on Earth,
for the Lord, the Messiah, has had his birth."

The sky was filled with angel's light
singing praises to God that holy night.

Glory to God in highest heaven above!
Peace to all people whom God does love.

The shepherds arose from their bended knee,
saying to each other, "Let us go and see!
Let us leave our flocks here in the cold
to find the baby of which we've been told."

The shepherds found that they were soon able
to find Mary and Joseph and the babe in the stable.
They told them all that they had seen and heard,
then going back, praised God for His holy Word.

The scene shifted when the night was done.
Joseph found a house for the mother and son.
They stayed in Bethlehem, the house of bread,
and were safe with nothing left to dread.

At the time of the birth, there shone a bright star,
which was seen by some sages in a country afar.
Journeying into Jerusalem, they ask for some news
of a child that was born King of the Jews.

At that time, over Judea, Herod did rule,
a king most jealous and vicious and cruel.
When he met those sages, his jealousy caught fire,
but he said, "To worship the baby is my only desire."

Herod summoned the priests and the scribes of the law
to search the scriptures and tell what they saw.
They found in the book of the Prophet Micah
that a ruler would rise from Bethlehem in Judah.

MILNE'S MUSINGS

"Go find him and come tell me, my homage. I'll pay,"
said crafty King Herod, sending them on their way.
To their joy, they were led to Bethlehem town
as light from a star shone brightly down.

Finding the house, they knelt before
the child whom they had come to adore—.
To this one they had so earnestly sought,
gold, frankincense and myrrh they brought.

When we read through the story, it always seems
to be filled with angels, visions, and dreams.
In a dream they were told to go home another way,
while Joseph was told to take the baby to Egypt to stay.

When those eastern sages did not return,
Herod's jealousy begins to blaze and burn.
To his soldiers he said, "It would give me great joy
to have you slaughter every first-born Bethlehem boy!"

Such is the story we remember this night.
a story of shepherds and a star shining bright;
a story of slaughter by Herod the King;
a story of what God, in Jesus, did bring!

Be this your thought at Christmas time,
as you ponder anew this story sublime:
what good does it do this story to trace
unless he is born in our time and place?

We've journeyed in faith over another year.
We've shared a smile; we've cried a tear.

But this we've learned in our struggle and strife,
Christmas means GOD IS WITH US through all our life.

Through the Eyes of Love

Even when we know that death is close at hand,
it leaves such a hole, and all that we planned
is not to be. Oft we think of what we should have done
or said, such as listened to our precious love who's gone.

But when death comes, unannounced, by their own hand,
it shatters our being. How and where, now, do we stand?
We blame ourselves. *Oh God, we should have known
and solved the problem before it came full blown.*

Why didn't they tell us about feelings they hid
and the secrets and all the things that they did?
What was the shame they never, never said
or the blame that they kept sealed in their head?

So oft we blame ourselves: *the fault is ours,*
or so our minds think in those restless hours.
If only they knew of the sheer devastation
that, by their own hand, was their creation.

This death was definitely not our choice.
God, help us to hear that small, still inner voice

telling us, over and over again, "You are not alone!"
They would have stopped it, had they known.

From those who have tried the suicide route
but lived and have told us what it's all about,
we've learned that always self-worth's at the base,
and if they were gone there'd be a smile on each face.

They thought that they were the problem, an obsession;
seeking a way out became their chief mission.
If only they'd have talked, a whisper or a shout,
for people who can help are around and about.

We can go to God with our troubles and strife,
for God in Christ came to share our human life.
Though some churches wouldn't bury under "holy" sod,
that was a human rule; it didn't come from God.

Four men came to Jesus. They carried a crippled friend
lying on a mat. His legs and back wouldn't flex or bend.
Jesus was in a house, and it was so full
they couldn't get through—push or pull.

So, they climbed on the roof and then a hole they made.
With ropes and his mat, they lowered him till at Jesus feet
he laid.
Jesus saw the faith of his friends above
and looked at the man through his eyes of love.

Jesus looked at the man, past the crippled muscle and bone,
seeing what the man feared: sins for which he couldn't atone.
But Jesus could and said, "My son, your sins are forgiven."

MILNE'S MUSINGS

The Pharisees were mad, saying that was strictly forbidden.

That story that Mark tells shows that Jesus knew
all the inner troubles and strife we don't show.
There is an old hymn, the words I'm sure you know:
"What a friend we have in Jesus," is the way it goes.

A Tale of Two Farmers

Down in a valley, so wide, steep and deep,
lived a poor farmer with only a few sheep.
The valley was floored with clay and stone;
the grass was sparse; the sheep mainly bone.
A few paltry acres were seeded to wheat,
but it wasn't enough for a grasshopper to eat.

A stagnant stream wandered side to side;
the taste of the water none could abide.
The run-off in spring was the only flow,
not like the torrent from long ages ago.
Quick melting glaciers carved through the loam
to clay and stone beneath the farmer's home.

We've looked at the bottom, now to the top
where the other farmer had a bumper crop.
The soil was rich. The rains came on time.
Never on his wheat was there a frosty rime.
Owning from the valley as far as he could see,
he said to himself, "This is how I want to be."

Though he was rich, he never turned greedy.
He always helped the poor and the needy.
One day he walked to the valley's rim.
Looking below, he saw a situation grim.
His crop was turning a bright harvest gold,
but hail had turned the other's crop to mold.

How can I help? was his very first thought.
I've had it lucky. He's sweat, and he's fought!
All his hard work has brought him no gain.
Even from here, I see his heartache and pain.
I really must think before I go off to sleep
of how I can help him in this valley so deep.

How can I help? I don't know his name!
If I don't try, I'll always carry the blame!
If I did something, my conscience would clear,
and before God and men I'd have nothing to fear.
Yes, yes, that is how I'll make his life better!
I'll ask him to work for me. I'll send him a letter!

He sat at a table with pen and with ink
His words just flowed without having to think.
"I farm just above you. I've seen your plight,
and I want to do something, if that's alright.
I want you to come and work for me.
I also have a place for your whole family."

He folded his letter, filling an envelope green,
hoping his letter soon would be seen.
He was so excited, he couldn't wait till day,

so he ran to the rim to throw his letter away.
Since it was a bright moonlit night,
he watched as his letter floated out of sight.

Well, would you believe the very next day,
the poor farmer was out early on his way
to find some pasture for his starving flock.
There on the gravel path, on top of a rock,
lay the letter in its beautiful envelope green.
Said the farmer, "That's the prettiest envelope I've ever seen!"

Picking it up, to his house he quickly ran,
calling his family, "Come as fast as you can.
Come see this treasure that I have just found!
Aren't we the luckiest family around!
Let's put the beautiful envelope green
by the mantel clock, so it can always be seen"

Here was their chance for a new, better life
away from the back-breaking toil and strife.
They looked at the beauty from the outside,
ignoring the message, it carried sealed inside.
The letter-writer waited and waited in vain,
thinking his message must be lost—a thought that caused him
much pain.

The other's plight was burned on his heart.
He decided what was needed - a new start.
He wrote the same letter. Now with a prayer,
he hoped that his letter soon would be there.
He sealed his letter in an envelope blue,

Hoping and praying that it would get through.

One of the children was skipping in the yard.
Seeing blue on the gravel was not too hard.
Taking the envelope, she ran on flying feet.
She wanted her family to share this blue treat.
Yes, it, too, went to the treasured mantelpiece.
Unseen went the letter that would bring release.

Disappointed, the author would try once again,
for he wanted that family to be free of the pain.
The words of the letter remained the same,
if only he knew the other man's full name!
The letter was sealed in the brightest gold.
Maybe this time the message would unfold.

For a tomato from one of the scraggly plants
the mother was searching when at a glance
at the dried-up peas. Look and behold!
There was an envelope of the purest gold.
Joy and excitement, now they had three:
the most beautiful envelopes there ever could be.

He must find a way! The farmer scratched his head;
he rolled and tossed on his beautiful bed.
Sleep was elusive. He still needed a plan
that would offer hope to the other man.
A hand he desperately wanted to give
to the farmer in the valley so he could live.

MILNE'S MUSINGS

From his son's bedroom down the hall,
he heard his soft breathing rise and fall.
There was his answer, it was so clear,
message and the messenger were near.
Sleep closed his eyes for on the morrow
he knew how to ease the other's sorrow.

After their breakfast, the father and son
went to the porch facing the morning sun.
"Son, now of you a favor I must ask.
I want you to engage in an important task.
Climb down the valley to the family and say,
'My father wants you to work for him today.'"

Now, my friends, I am sorry to have to say
that's the end of the story that came my way.
Did the two farmers become true friends?
I don't know. That was how the story ends.
But this I must say ere we leave this place,
think of God's dealing with our human race.

God's love is revealed in Earth's mantle green.
New poplar leaves are the nicest I've seen.
Green the wheat's new growth on the farm.
Green of our riders, our provincial charm.
Green the pasture as calves gambol and play.
Will we ever listen to what green letters say?

God gave us the blue in the arch of the sky
and the blue of love in some people's eye.
The blue of lakes nestled in forest green

make the loveliest landscapes to be seen.
Will we humans see that God's letters abound?
For when we open our eyes, many are found.

Fields of Canola in bright golden bloom,
ripe wheat awaiting the combine's boom,
a golden harvest, moon lighting the earth—
these are just some golden things, for what it's worth.
The golden pages of our sacred book
are golden letters, if we care to look.

Words from the Psalmists are golden also,
and the Prophets told us the right way to go.
When God's letters were mainly ignored,
God still wants the relationship restored.
God sent His son to come down to Earth.
In a stable in Bethlehem, he had his birth.

He came to live God's love and to share
that love to all people, burdened with care,
like the farmer and family who were so poor.
They needed God's love, that's for sure.
The rich also needed the gift of God's grace.
In God's gracious love, we all have our place.

Christ is with us when we carry heavy loads.
In our ease and contentment, the Spirit goads
us to share what God's grace has provided
till the fruits of the earth are equally divided.
God is with us in Creator, in Spirit, and son.
In all times and places, God loves everyone.

Water From Our Well

Do you remember a year long gone by?
when hope arose with clouds in the sky?
They, like the earth, were parched and dry.
The wind blew them away, leaving a tear in your eye.

Not so, this year: every cloud meant rain!
Your prayer was for sunshine, again, again.
The rain didn't come as a gentle shower;
downpours were measured in inches per hour.

We all have stories of rivers and lakes, of water and wells.
Some wells, like sloughs, hold water that smells.
Jeremiah says that God is like fresh, clear water from a spring,
But God's people dig cisterns, cracked and holding nothing.

I'm going to tell you of water from a well on our farm.
We all drank from it. Surely, it did us no harm.
Salesmen would stop by on hot summer days.
"It's so hot. May I have some water?" they would say.

My dad would warn them of that clear water's power.
"If you have a glassful, it will stay with you less than an hour."

"But I'm so dry and hot. I'll just take a sip."
Then the glass would be empty, not even a drip.

"I'll have another with its crystal-clear taste."
Mom called us for lunch. We'd no time to waste.
Our guest was seated the closest to the door.
Mom had seen what happened many times before.

Grace was said, and the food passed around.
Cutlery scaping china was the only sound.
In the semi-silence, we heard a gurgle then a rumble
as all the food in his stomach started to tumble.

The look on his face showed surprise, horror, and fear.
Was his demise from the water so very near?
Out the door, to the privy, he made a mad dash.
His face now the colour of water-soaked ash.

Mom knew the drill; she sent hot water, soap, and a towel,
hoping that he had not torn a hole in his bowel.
Now the laughs on auld Scottie; he sold the old place.
He should have bottled that water, giving the Fleet enema
a race
or the runs, if you'd pardon the pun.
Then I would be rich, and we would have fun.

Thanksgiving! How?

Next Monday is special; it's Thanksgiving Day!
Now, Lord, about that, I have got a lot to say.
In the world and our lives, we see great strife.
How can we give thanks for this trouble-filled life?

Our cost-of-living rockets through the roof.
Look at our bank account, if you need proof.
When we think about life, no matter how we try,
All that comes out is a great sorrowful sigh.

Our unemployment statistics are far too high.
Some cannot find a job, hard though they try.
Welfare rolls grow; food banks are busy.
Our whole society is thrown into a tizzy.

Statistics are numbers. We must bear in mind
That each unemployed is one of our kind.
A woman, a man, an eager youth—
Each number's a person, and that's the truth!

Cancer, stroke, diabetes, kidney, and heart
Are some of the diseases that tear us apart,

Taking our loved ones. So, we are left alone,
And once tender hearts are turned into stone.

Cancer devours a precious young life,
Taking a father, a husband, a mother, a wife.
Bad accidents strike so many of our young,
Maiming or killing the strong.

When for an illness we find a new cure,
Then we find a new illness, that's for sure!
The cost of health care goes right out of sight,
Leaving us here in this horrible plight.

Businesses are closing all over our town.
Some just open up and then they're shut down.
Each padlocked door holds a shattered dream.
Things get worse and worse, so it would seem.

And, God, when we look at the world scen,
It is probably the worst that it's ever been.
ISIS, beheadings, and terror lead to despair!
How can we celebrate this holiday fair?

Is our country strong? Will it last?
Or is it dying? Is it failing fast?
And in the United States, if they elect Trump,
Their economy and ours will be a sliding slump.

It's not just our nation, God, look at the world,
With the flags of war again being unfurled.
Now Syria is a painful festering sore.
For decade upon decade, they've been at war.

MILNE'S MUSINGS

Drought, floods, tornadoes, and plane crashes,
Our lives now seem like a mouth full of ashes.
Through it all, Lord, you show no action.
Your inactivity drives us to distraction.

Thanksgiving comes, but we've little to show
That would counterbalance our great tale of woe.
How can we give thanks? Our world is so gray
With sickness and sorrow that's here to stay.

Lord, these are the things placed on our plate.
Our lives, as you know, are in a sorry state.
How can we pause now in thanksgiving
In the midst of this awful life we're living?

In the world without and our lives within,
Our long list of woes creates a dreadful din.
Pain and suffering, agony, guilt and fear—
Oh Lord, our Lord, please hear! PLEASE HEAR!

Hear now, oh Lord, our bitter cry!
How can you stand so silently by?
How can we give you thanks and praise
When we are lost in this maddening maze?

In Egypt of old, you heard the slaves' cry!
To Moses and Aaron your presence was nigh.
Through poet and prophet your word was spoken.
Now, in this service, let your silence be broken!

I heard the Lord speak in the depths of my being,
Saying to me, "Open your eyes! Now, start seeing!

I will speak again to you, oh man.
Open your ears as best as you can.
You say that in trouble, I really don't care,
But I want you to listen, becoming aware.

"Listen, oh my people, now listen and hear.
In all of your troubles, I've always been near.
My people of old walked through the Red Sea,
Walking in faith for they couldn't see me.

"In the beginning, I created you free.
In my love I gave you opportunity
To obey or disobey, to do good or ill,
And, oh my people, you disobey still!

"Of all my creation, I made you, alone, to be
The only creature able to create like me.
Female and male to share equally together—
See how you've tried to subdue one another?

"I have given you life in a bountiful land,
With riches abundant from my gracious hand.
All I asked was that first you would give
A portion to others, so they also could live.

"See how you've used my precious gift,
Twixt rich and poor to create a great rift.
Blessings you take from my bountiful store
Yet cry out in greed for more and more.

"I never told you that I would try
To make your life sail smoothly by.

MILNE'S MUSINGS

This, I promised—this is most true—
In the storms of life, I'll never leave you!

"Though your troubles in life may blaze like a fire,
To have flames consume you was not my desire.
But as the hot, fiery furnace refines the ore,
I want good character to come to the fore.

"Prophets I sent, sent to speak my word,
You silenced them; they were not heard.
My servants were rejected, enduring pain.
This happened again and again and again.

"When at the last I came to Earth in a life
Again, I was met with rejection and strife;
In Jesus I came to live out my care;
On the cross, you stripped Him bare!

"My love and power were shown in resurrection,
Where I showed you forgiveness not rejection.
See, oh my people, see my presence in pain.
Know that, in love, I will always sustain.

"You ask in the midst of your long tale of woe
How I expect your thanksgiving to show.
How easy you look for all that is wrong;
How quickly you sing me your very sad song.

"To the sadness in your life, your eyes are turned.
All the sadness of the world on my heart is burned.
You want me to erase trouble with a wave of my hand
And, like magic, once more make a perfect land.

Rev Don Milne B.A. M.S.T.

"I made the world perfect, and I made you free.
You are free to live in greed or in charity.
I gave you time: time for killing or healing,
A time for tearing down or a time for building.

The only way my creation can be restored whole
Is when love for my world burns deep in your soul.
To help you live in compassion and love,
I sent you my Spirit on wings, like a dove.

"Look at your life, like a beach full of sand.
Hold the magnet of gratitude fast in your hand.
That magnet finds all the metals of blessing
That your greedy hand is always missing."

I heard God's questions in the depths of my being,
And like Job had to move from hearing to seeing.
No, I never saw God; I saw what God had done
In creation and redemption through Jesus, the son.

In silence God asks us to sift through our life,
Sift through the disaster, the trouble, the strife
And find, there, the seeds that are waiting release:
Seeds of compassion and justice and peace.

God planted those seeds in the depths of our soul,
Asking that we would let God's justice begin to roll,
Roll like the river that floods over the earth,
That peace, justice, and compassion would all have their birth.

Christ's Last Temptation

After we had eaten, I led them out
to a lonely garden. No one was about.
There I asked them to sit and stay
while I went farther, alone, to pray.

I asked Peter, James, and John—the three—
to come farther into the garden with me.
Maybe in these, my three-special friends,
I'd find the strength that friendship lends.

They didn't know the night's gathering gloom
had brought to my spirit a deepening doom.
I, who had made others healthy and whole,
had in that time the dark night of the soul.

**"The sorrow in my heart is so great that it
almost crushes me. Stay here and keep watch
with me."**

In the garden, I am all alone—alone
in anguish of spirit to which humans are prone.
If it be possible, Father, take this cup away,

for my life is good and I want to stay.

Life is good. I am young and strong
with so much to do as I journey along.
There are lessons to teach and lives to heal
and people to make open to think and feel.

I have my hopes and unfulfilled dreams.
Even for me time is so short it seems.
I need more time to do what I must:
to show people love and build up their trust.

Father, if it is possible, let me live,
for I have only this on life to give.
I have been faithful. I have been good.
And I will do what you think I should.

**"My father, if it is possible, take this cup of
suffering from me. Yet not what I want, but
what you want."**

I will go back, rejoining my friends.
Much human strength on friendship depends.
Oh no! All asleep! Not one of them alert
to watch with me in my anguish and hurt!

**"How is it that you three were not able to keep
watch with me for even one hour? Keep watch
and pray that you will not fall into temptation.
The spirit is willing, but the flesh is weak."**

MILNE'S MUSINGS

My disciples slept! They heard me ask
what shouldn't have been a difficult task:
to watch and pray for me as alone I go
to gain some strength for this night of woe.

How easy they slept. Yet in their hands
the fate of my mission falls or stands.
They are so weak. They are not strong.
They need my presence to bear them along.

My father, I love them, and they love me.
I think of how unhappy they soon will be.
Oh God, because they really don't know you,
they will not know how, my death, to view.

My friends and disciples will be so lost
when alone in the tempest they are tossed.
I need more time, maybe only a year,
then for their faith I'd have nothing to fear.

I tried to prepare them, I really did,
but Peter acted like a spoiled little kid.
"God forbit it, Lord! This must never happen to you!"
He wouldn't listen, though my words were true.

This experience is so very new!
What, oh God my God, shall I do?
They'll be lost. I am young. I love this life.
Give me more strength to face my strife.

I know that if longer I were to remain
it would not lessen their parting pain.

I know that, for me, that time is now.
God, give me strength. Show me how.

**"My father, if this cup of suffering cannot be
taken away unless I drink it, your will be done."**

See them there, all fast asleep,
each one like a little lost sheep!
Oh God, how I love them, and they love me.
How broken-hearted they are going to be.

Oh God, my father, there must be another way,
the vastness of your love thus to portray.
This cup of death, now let it be gone!
Let there be life for me, your son!

Oh God, why should I die on a cross of pain?
Why should your son ever be beaten and slain?
Could you not, in a flash of light,
reveal yourself in your creative might.

Through the deep darkness of the human soul,
let your light, like Ezekiel's chariot, roll.
Then they could see; it would be all plain.
They all would acknowledge you as God again.

What of their choice? But it would free me!
Why is human freedom so important to Thee?
Why must they see in your only son
Isaiah's silent, serving, suffering one?

This battle's done; my temptation goes away.
Will it return with the light of day?
There on the cross, before I'm dead
will temptation again raise its ugly head?

**"My father, if this cup of suffering cannot be
taken away unless I drink it, your will be done."**

I must wake my friends. The flesh is weak.
After tonight, I know whereof I speak.
Yonder through the shades of night
I see approaching torches burning bright.

My time has come. I must now go.
Now is the time for courage and faith to show!
Now I must go to receive a kiss
from Judas, whose love I truly miss.

**"Are you still sleeping and resting? Look! The
hour has come for the son of man to be handed
over to the power of sinful men. Get up; let
us go. Look, here is the man who is betraying me!"**

Now, oh my God, it's just as I thought;
how quickly they forget all that I taught.
One of my friends has his sword in his hand,
trying through violence to make his stand.

"Put your sword back in its place."

Stay with me, God, through the rest of this night.
I know they are wrong; they think they are right.

Let them beat and revile, humiliate in rage.
Wrong won't be victorious at the end of the age.

Let them have fun, as they play with that crown
and with great derision, humbly bow down.
Let them spit in my face, yelling, "Who's the one?"
Give me the strength to show that we have won!

Strengthen me as they hammer that nail,
and on the cross, my feet they impale.
My seamless robe they protect and save
while tearing apart this temple you gave.

Oh God, my father, they heard me often speak
that when you're wronged, turn the other cheek.
Now as I hang in this awful pain,
help me to make real those words again.

**"Forgive them, Father! They don't know what they
are doing."**

Their taunts and jeers are hard to bear,
but the hardest of all, "Come down from there
and we will believe!" Yet I now hear
a word of support from one whose death also is near.

Then, in quiet penitential reverence,
without any claim in his own defense,
"Jesus, when you're through this awful hour,
remember me when you come in your kingly power."

"I promise you that today you will be in paradise with me."

There's my mother, who gave me life
and supported me in my childhood strife,
standing broken-hearted, weeping.
She gave her life into my keeping.

My brothers, now, can leave her alone,
because she stayed with me at this convict's throne.
She gave me care as only a mother can give!
How can I help her yet to live?

Ah, there is John. His love drew him near.
I'm sure he'd look after my mother dear.
God, let your strength be with me still
that aloud I may speak a testamentary will.

"He is your son. She is your mother."

I taught about flowers, that you painted each part.
I spoke of the birds, that you loved each little heart.
Before in my need you always were there.
Oh God who has gone, please answer my prayer!

I lift up mine eyes, but you are not there.
I look to the hills; they point to despair.
Downwards I look, seeing only the curious stare.
While deep inside I find a strange hollowness there.

Where have you gone, oh God of my youth?
I cannot feel your power or your truth.
Why have you left me, oh great God above?

I have only this emptiness, not your peace and love.

"*Eloi, eloi, lema sabachthani?* My God, my God, why did you abandon me?"

All my muscles and sinews are stretched and taut.
The sun's hot furnace makes my fevered brow hot.
Inside I feel like Shadrach's and Meshach's place.
Is there no compassion left in the whole human race?

"I am thirsty."

It's not just the wine that brought its release.
A kind act of sharing has brought me some peace.
Oh, I had worried that it was all for naught
that I had lived, preached, healed and taught.

That kindly act of a lifted drink
made me remember, made me think
of what I had said when their roads I trod:
that a kind act to a person is also to God.
God, you sent me here with my human face
to show your love to the whole human race.
Now one of them has reversed the role,
restoring my faith and making me whole.

It was not wasted! Today, I have not lost!
From despair to faith my spirit has crossed.
All my work is accomplished in the acts of today.
Oh God, give me strength that aloud I may say,

MILNE'S MUSINGS

"It is finished!"

All through my life, as I lay down to sleep,
I prayed to you, Lord, my spirit to keep.
You were there in the quiet, nothing could me harm,
and it was the same in the boat during that raging storm.

I'm now at the end of this varied life:
a life full of joy that ended in strife.
Lord God, give me strength to aloud pray
and for the very list time from my heart say,

"Father, in your hands I place my spirit!"

REMEMBRANCE

What Is A Veteran?

He's a man who looks the world straight in the eye. She's a woman who feels an extra heart-tug when the flag goes by. He's a man who stands a little straighter when the national anthem is played. She's a woman who steps a little faster when a marching tune is played. They are veterans!

They come in all different sizes, shapes, and colors: big, small, short, tall, skinny, fat, black, brown, and white. They are women, and they are men. In total, they speak almost every language under the sun. They come from almost every ethnic background to be found on this planet, and they are proud of what their parents were, but they faithfully and with true patriotism, served their new country. They are Canadians. They are veterans.

They were riding the rails and crisscrossing the country in search of a job, hungry, clothes in tatters, with cardboard insoles to cover the holes in their shoes. Joining up gave them boots and clothes, dignity and purpose instead of being a beggar. They were students, leaving the classrooms with high ideals of patriotism and service. They never left Canadian soil, serving as trainers and instructors to those who left to fight on foreign soil. They have many medals, showing all the areas of conflict where they served. They are veterans.

They are still fit and strong, strengthened and hardened like steel—the crucibles of battle like the foundry furnaces that turned the soft ingots of iron into steel. They are frail and ailing—their bodies wracked with pain all because they were the victims of the atrocities of war. They were too young, hiding their true age. They were middle-aged, not too old but no longer young. They are veterans!

They are Army, Navy, and Air Force. They are gunners and pilots, mechanics and clerks, sonar operators and tank commanders, and all in between. They are privates and generals, majors and corporals, petty officers and flying officers, and all the other ranks. They are regular members of the Canadian Armed Forces and the Reserves. They are citizen soldiers, volunteering in response to Canada's call. They are veterans.

They are gentiles and Jews, Catholics and Protestants, Atheists and believers. They are rich, and they are poor, and everywhere in between. They live in mansions at the lake and in shacks across the tracks. They live on First Nations reserves and on farms, in tiny hamlets and large cities. She anxiously waits on the widow's walk on the rooftop of her home for her fisherman husband to return. He anguishes every time his Mounted Police wife is called out at night. They are veterans!

They are conservative, liberal, and NDP. They vote for the best candidate and on the issues facing our society. They are proud of their Canadian past, alert to the Canadian present, and have a cautious confidence in Canada's future. They are good citizens who always get out to vote. They are veterans.

She marvels at the vast arch of the prairie skies. He likes the majesty of the Canadian mountains. They like the tranquility of the forest and the bustle of the cities. She likes the vast panorama of the prairies. He marvels at the ripple of water over a beaver dam and the roar of Niagara Falls. They are veterans.

She likes the happy sound of children at play. He is glad that his grandchildren can play "Hide and Seek" as a game and not as the reality of their daily lives. She is the first person to bring food to a neighbor when there is a tragedy. He is the first to volunteer to help in times of need and the last to come home. They are veterans.

She has the quiet dignity of the person who knows the price of freedom. He has the clear eyes of a person who respects himself. She is courage living on Main Street. He is patriotism mowing his lawn on a Saturday afternoon. They are justice and equality with open minds. They are veterans.

They are peace-loving people who know the price of war. They are comrades with ties to each other, stronger than blood, forged in the crucibles of battle.

They bear the scars of battle: some are visible, constant reminders of the harsh cruelty of war. They bear the scars of battle: unseen, invisible, burned indelibly on their mind and spirit. They are good, patriotic community leaders who became citizen soldiers at their country's call. They are volunteers. They are veterans.

In their secret heart there is always a spot of sorrow, a souvenir of sadness for lost and departed comrades. In their eyes a tear, as silently they stand at the somber cenotaph, watching the wreaths of memory and tribute being laid. He is Canada with an honorable discharge. She is democracy with a good conduct medal hidden away in the darkness of a keepsake box. They are freedom, holding high the torch that they caught, the torch thrown by their falling comrades who made the ultimate sacrifice. They are veterans. They are veterans!

Lest We Forget

The eleventh hour of the eleventh day of the eleventh month in 1918 was when the combatants agreed to lay down their weapons to end the First World War. Veterans used the day, Armistice Day, to remember their fallen comrades. Now there are no veterans of that war still living. When the Second World War broke out, the name of the day had to be changed to Remembrance Day. The veterans of that war are getting older and fewer each year. For that reason, there are people who want to do away with Remembrance Day. Also, they say that the emphasis is on war and it should be on peace. I believe that we focus on peace, but we also need to remember that peace has a price, a costly price. We need to remember, honour, and give thanks to those people who voluntarily gave up their lives for the freedom and liberty of others. We do that by honouring and giving thanks to our veterans.

We need to remember the past to know the present and plan for the future. I think that G.K. Chesteron was right when he wrote, "The disadvantage of people not knowing the past is that they do not know the present. History is a hill or high point of vantage from which alone people see the town in which they live or the age in which they are living."

It is so easy to dismiss the past as being unimportant for our present and future. Sometimes we try to forget because of the pain of the past, but we ignore the past at our own peril and repeat the mistakes of our ancestors if we do not remember. A few years ago, the late Elie Wiesel was awarded the Nobel Peace Prize. He was a Jew who saw most of his family put to death in Hitler's concentration death camps. He survived Auschwitz, eventually coming to North America to live. He was a good writer, having written many books about the Holocaust. He believed that we must never be allowed to forget the horror of it all and the depths of depravity to which humanity can sink. In our individual lives, and in the larger life of society, only when we truly remember can we deal with the horror that often lies hidden beneath the surface. Only when the past is dealt with openly and honestly can we begin to build or rebuild the bridges between peoples that have been blown apart by conflict. Then, and only then, can we truly work for peace and reconciliation.

But it is not just a matter of remembering; what we remember is also important. As we grow older, our memory tends to retain only those things that were helpful and hopeful, satisfying and splendid. The sordid and less wholesome things tend to get lost. We say that time heals, but that is only because our conscious memory is so selective. We cannot be allowed to remember only the bits we like or grow nostalgic for the past we remember as a result of our built-in selection process.

What do we remember today? Not victory, for in wars there is no victor. All of us are diminished by war and conflict. Yes, one side may come out on top, but at the cost of tremendous losses. What we remember today is people: brave people and fear-ridden people, courageous people and misguided people. We remember that events like the Holocaust were not merely an error in human judgement but the result of deliberate planning, or in theological terms, our human sin. It was the culmination of human depravity and evil. Today we remember that any or all of us are capable of similar things. There, but for the grace of God, go I.

Remembering, we give thanks that there were people of courage and bravery who saw what was happening to people, who saw the loss of freedom and liberty and the rise of oppression, who took arms to eradicate that evil. Bravely and courageously, they adopted the awful means of war to put an end to what they saw as a greater evil. They did what they felt to be right for the cause of peace, justice, liberty, and love. Today we remember, and remembering, we pray that the blood-soaked lessons of history will never be repeated. We remember, lest we forget.

Rudyard Kipling wrote:*

The tumult and the shouting dies;
The Captains and the Kings depart:
Still stands Thine ancient sacrifice,
A humble and a contrite heart.
Lord God of Hosts, be with us yet,
Lest we forget—lest we forget.

***Recessional by Rudyard Kipling 1897
for Queen Victoria's diamond jubilee**

HYMNS

Oh God of Vast Creation

Tune Lancashire 7676D

Of earth and stars of space,
we come with adoration,
your way of love to trace.
You called a pilgrim people
to leave their home of old;
to Abraham and Sarah
you made your way unfold.

Oh God of great redemption,
in love you heard the cry
of slaves for liberation.
Your presence still was nigh.
A star shone bright above us;
you walked the earth below;v
for in the Christ Incarnate
you came your love to show.

Oh God of grace and glory,
Oh God of space and time,
we hear again the story

of suffering love sublime.
We have your Spirit's presence
in gathering here today,
as in this holy temple
we pause to praise and pray.

God of each generation,
we offer you our song
of praise and adoration.
Your grace has made us strong.
We thank you for the history
of faithful prayer and praise!
We pray that you will guide us
through all our coming days.

The Silent Stones

Tune 8686 Dunfermline Common Meter

The silent stones should sing a song
if all around are still,
so Jesus praised the chanting throng
as he rode up the hill.

The broken palms were waved on high
and laid as carpet green.
The passion of our Lord is nigh;
His glory soon is seen.

The silent stones should sing their song
if now we all are still.
We see our master ride along
to die on Calvary's hill.

Break now your foolish stiff-necked pride;
bow in humility.
Christ takes his lowly suffering ride
to reign eternally.

MEDITATIONS

Flowers of Earth and Buds of Heaven

Words do not come easy at a time like this, and if they did, they would be too glib and facetious. We all have questions as to why some little ones are born with so many strikes against them. There are no easy answers. The only thing that I can say with real assurance and honesty is that, along with the love that she had from her family, Shantel was equally loved by God, and now she is at home in God's presence. Jesus told us that we should never despise a little child and that their angels are always in the presence of God. One of the two recorded times when Jesus' anger blazed was when his disciples sent away the people who were bringing children to Jesus. Then, after rebuking his followers, he took the children in his arms and blessed them.

When Jesus called himself the Good Shepherd, he said that he came among us that we might have life—life in all its fullness. I believe that for Shantel that fullness or completeness of life has her now running, laughing, and playing in the greater world of God's presence. Another family who had a similar experience in the illness and death of their infant son gave me a poem to read at their son's service. I want to share that poem, now, a poem that many of you know.

*The Rose Beyond the Wall

Near shady wall a rose once grew,
Budded and blossomed in God's free light,
Watered and fed by morning dew,
Shedding its sweetness day and night.

As it grew and blossomed fair and tall,
Slowly rising to loftier height,
It came to a crevice in the wall
Through which there shone a beam of light.

Onward it crept with added strength
With never a thought of fear or pride,
It followed the light through the crevice's length
And unfolded itself on the other side.

The light, the dew, the broadening view
Were found the same as they were before,
And it lost itself in beauties new,
Breathing its fragrance more and more.

Shall claim of death cause us to grieve
And make our courage faint and fall?

Nay! Let us faith and hope receive—
The rose still grows beyond the wall,

Scattering fragrance far and wide
Just as it did in days of yore,
Just as it did on the other side,
Just as it will forevermore.

—A.L. Frink

A five-year-old boy, with his mother's help, had worked for weeks to make his father a surprise Christmas gift: a beautiful vase for his office. When it was finished, they decorated it with a ribbon and placed it out of sight, behind the Christmas tree, where it would not only be hidden but protected from breakage. The boy was very excited about his secret. Finally, Christmas morning dawned and the family gathered about the tree. The boy took the vase from its hiding place and ran to his father. In his excitement he stumbled and the vase slipped form his hands, falling on the rocker of a rocking chair and shattering into a hundred pieces. They boy burst into tears over what had happened and the loss he experienced. His father, trying to console the heartbroken boy, said, "Son, don't cry. Thank you for the gift, but its' not worth crying about. Don't you worry a thing about it."

Fortunately, the mother had more perception and understanding. She took her son in her arms and said, "Of course, it was important! We worked so hard on it!" And she cried with her son. Finally, when his tears had subsided, she said, "Son, let's pick up the pieces and make something of them."

It's normal and natural to cry. It is crucial to weep, because Shantel mattered. She was so special. And she is special and important to God, as well. God knows your sorrow, for God also had a child die—his son. Knowing that Shantel is safe and secure in God's loving presence, we must pick up the pieces and make something of them. May God grant us all His strength as we pick up the pieces.

*The Rose Still Grows Beyond the Wall. Poetry by A.L. Frink for a collection of poetry by A.L. Frink

A Prayer for Shantel Brown

Scarcely gone the winter snows
Ere the crocus blooming grows.
First the bud and then the flower,
All nature reveals God's creative power

Some reach not full, glorious bloom
Ere some disaster sees their doom.
Every child is a gift of love
From God, our creator, up above.

To us, in love, each is given
Flowers of earth and buds of heaven.
They teach us, if we could see,
How this world is meant to be.

Into this world with struggle and strife
Shantel was given this time of life.
She gave her smiles; her lesson was clear:
Each moment of life is precious and dear.
While no more we see this bud of rose,
In the garden of God, a full flower she grows.

Dear Reader

Thank you, dear reader, for persevering through to the end of this last sermon and prayer. I hope and pray that this book has been a blessing to you. May God bless you and keep you, in Jesus' name we pray. Amen.

—Don

ACKNOWLEDGEMENTS

I did not know the cost of writing even a collection like this—costly in energy, time, and money. Thank you to my family, who made me realize how big our family is. They have all been supportive, sharing important suggestions and ideas. To Cheryl and Ken, Dale and Eleanor, Doug and Moira, and all the grandkids and great-grandkids, thank you for your encouragement and support. To the following who helped me physically, Aaron Andrychuk, Dennis and Kathy Arbuthnott, Dale Milne, and the staff at College Park One and Two, for the support and help with the manuscript when I needed it, my sincere thanks.

To the people of the churches—Crane Valley, Cardross, Davyroyd, Manyberries, Atzikom, Ebenezer, Seven Persons, Bladworth and Chattam School, Bradwell, Clavet, and Floral—where I served during my college days as a student minister, thank you. Seamans, Punnichy, Raymore and Tait, North Battleford, Meadow Lake and Dorintosh, Westview and Orkney, where I served following my ordination, thank you. To the people of Yorkton Radar Station (later to become Whitespruce Youth Treatment Centre), thank you. I thank all of you for your support and long suffering under my ministry. I also thank my many colleagues and ministerial friends for their support and guidance over the years. I would be remiss if I didn't thank Molly Kitchen and her husband Bob for their review of these works and their kind words in the introduction.

Printed in Canada